DENVER NUGGETS

ALL-TIME GREATS

BY TED COLEMAN

Book design by Jake Slavik
Cover design by Jake Slavik

Photographs ©: David Zalubowski/AP Images, cover (top), 1 (top); Kirby Lee/AP Images, cover (bottom), 1 (bottom); Denver Post/Getty Images, 4; AP Images, 6; Mark Duncan/AP Images, 8; Focus On Sport/Getty Images Sport/Getty Images, 10; Susan Ragan/AP Images, 13; Al Messerschmidt Archive/AP Images, 15; Jack Dempsey/AP Images, 16; Chris Szagola/AP Images, 18; Jeff Chiu/AP Images, 20

Press Box Books, an imprint of Press Room Editions.

ISBN
978-1-63494-602-5 (library bound)
978-1-63494-620-9 (paperback)
978-1-63494-638-4 (epub)
978-1-63494-654-4 (hosted ebook)

Library of Congress Control Number: 2022913242

Distributed by North Star Editions, Inc.
2297 Waters Drive
Mendota Heights, MN 55120
www.northstareditions.com

Printed in the United States of America
Mankato, MN
012023

ABOUT THE AUTHOR

Ted Coleman is a freelance sportswriter and children's book author who lives in Louisville, Kentucky, with his trusty Affenpinscher, Chloe.

TABLE OF CONTENTS

CHAPTER 1

ROCKET START 4

CHAPTER 2

STRIKING GOLD 10

CHAPTER 3

NEW NUGGETS 16

TIMELINE 22

TEAM FACTS 23

MORE INFORMATION 23

GLOSSARY 24

INDEX 24

BECK
40
DENVER
40

CHAPTER 1

ROCKET START

Pro basketball teams had come and gone from Denver. The sport settled in Denver for good in 1967. The Denver Rockets featured a familiar face to local basketball fans. Center **Byron Beck** went right from the University of Denver to the Rockets.

After seven years, the Rockets became the Nuggets. Beck was there for ten seasons. Fans loved him. But he didn't put up huge numbers. Beck worked hard on the court. And he rarely missed games. The team improved quickly during his time in Denver.

THOMPSON

15

Dave Robisch was a similar player to Beck. The 6'10" center was a strong scorer under the basket. He also was a fierce rebounder.

The Rockets' top scorer during much of the early 1970s was **Ralph Simpson**. The guard put up 27.4 points per game in just his second season. He averaged nearly 20 per game in his Denver career.

Denver played its first eight seasons in the American Basketball Association (ABA). The ABA was known for a fun style of play. That was a perfect fit for guard **David Thompson**.

STAT SPOTLIGHT

POINTS IN A GAME

NUGGETS TEAM RECORD

David Thompson: 73 (April 9, 1978)

Thompson was nicknamed "Skywalker" for how he hung in the air. Thompson was an amazing athlete. He was also one of the league's best dunkers. He once shattered a backboard on a dunk.

The ABA merged with the NBA in 1976. The Nuggets had some early success in the NBA. Thompson and center **Dan Issel** led the way. Issel wasn't the high jumper that Thompson was. But he could score.

Issel was an accurate shooter from outside and inside. And he missed just 24 games over his 15 seasons. Behind the high-scoring duo, the Nuggets won their division in 1976–77. They won it again the next season. Both players' careers lasted into the 1980s. By then, Denver was ready for a new run of success.

LARRY BROWN

Point guard Larry Brown ended his playing career with the Denver Rockets in 1972. He then got into coaching. The Nuggets hired him as head coach in 1974. Brown led Denver to a team-record 65 wins in his first season. Brown won 65 percent of his games in five seasons. He would go on become the first coach to win both a college and NBA championship.

nuggets
ENGLISH
2

CHAPTER 2
STRIKING GOLD

In 1980, the Nuggets traded for **Alex English**. The forward hadn't played much in his first two NBA seasons. In Denver, English became one of the best scorers in league history.

English played 10 full seasons with the Nuggets. He made the All-Star team in eight. In all but one season he averaged more than 23 points per game. And he led the Nuggets to nine playoff appearances in a row.

English didn't do it alone. He, Dan Issel, and forward **Kiki VanDeWeghe** made up

STAT SPOTLIGHT

CAREER POINTS

NUGGETS TEAM RECORD

Alex English: 21,645

a strong scoring trio. VanDeWeghe twice had 50 points in a game.

Running the Denver offense was point guard **Lafayette "Fat" Lever**. Lever could do it all. He recorded 43 career triple-doubles in his career.

Guard **T. R. Dunn** was not a big scorer. Defense was his specialty. Dunn was one of the best defensive guards of the 1980s. He was a big rebounder. And his slick passing helped his teammates to score.

By the late 1980s, **Michael Adams** had taken over at point guard. Adams was reliable at the position. But in 1990–91 he blossomed

LEVER
12

into an elite scorer. He went from 15.5 points per game the previous season to 26.5. Adams's breakout season helped make up for the loss of English. He had left the year before.

Rookie point guard **Mahmoud Abdul-Rauf** came off the bench in 1990–91. Adams left that offseason. Abdul-Rauf took over as the full-time starter. He proved to be a talented scoring guard, too. Abdul-Rauf averaged at least 16 points per game in four seasons as a starter.

DOUG MOE

The 1980s Nuggets were often exciting, high-scoring teams. One of the reasons for that was coach Doug Moe. Moe wanted running and quick passes. It was all about taking as many shots as possible. Moe left with the most wins in team history. He led the Nuggets to the playoffs in each of his nine full seasons.

The 1990s Nuggets didn't win a lot of games. Center **Dikembe Mutombo** played some dominant defense, though. He spent his first five seasons with Denver. In 1995, he was named Defensive Player of the Year. Mutombo became one of the best shot blockers in NBA history. After a block, he famously wagged his finger to tell opponents "No."

NUGGETS
15
ANTHONY
15

CHAPTER 3

NEW NUGGETS

The Nuggets drafted **Antonio McDyess** in 1995. The forward ended up playing six seasons for Denver over two stints. He was at his best in the 2000–01 season, where he averaged more than 20 points and 12 rebounds.

The Nuggets traded McDyess a year later and in return got center **Marcus Camby**. Like Dikembe Mutombo, Camby blocked a lot of shots. He also won Defensive Player of the Year in 2006–07.

The 2000s Nuggets ran through **Carmelo Anthony**. Denver picked him third in the 2003 draft. The forward quickly proved to be a top scorer. His arrival began a 10-year playoff streak in Denver. Anthony stayed for the first seven. He never averaged fewer than 20 points per game. A lot of those points came on turnaround jump shots.

Running the offense at point guard was **Andre Miller**. His crafty passing set up his teammates to score. Meanwhile, **Nenê** was a strong presence under either basket. The center was a nightmare for defenders from close range. And he grabbed a lot of rebounds. Nenê was one of Denver's leaders for 10 years.

Miller was a pass-first point guard. **Jamal Murray** brought different skills to the position. Murray became the Nuggets' starter in the 2017–18 season. He could score in bunches. He scored 50 points twice in a 2020 playoff series against the Utah Jazz.

STAT SPOTLIGHT

SINGLE-SEASON FIELD-GOAL PERCENTAGE

NUGGETS TEAM RECORD

Nenê: .615 (2010-11)

15
dialpad
KINGS
30
JOKIC
15

The Nuggets didn't need Murray to run the offense. They had one of basketball's top weapons in **Nikola Jokic**. A center, Jokic did more than play near the basket. The 6'11" Jokic could score from anywhere. He was also a great passer. All those skills earned Jokic the Most Valuable Player (MVP) in 2021. He was the first NBA MVP in Nuggets history. He won the MVP again in 2022.

The Nuggets enjoyed success under Murray and Jokic. In 2020, the team reached the conference finals. Fans hoped their MVP could soon take them even further.

GEORGE KARL

Only two Nuggets coaches have won Coach of the Year. Doug Moe won in 1988. George Karl followed in 2013. Karl had a very similar run of success to Moe. He won 423 games in nine seasons. He also led the team to the 2009 conference finals.

TIMELINE

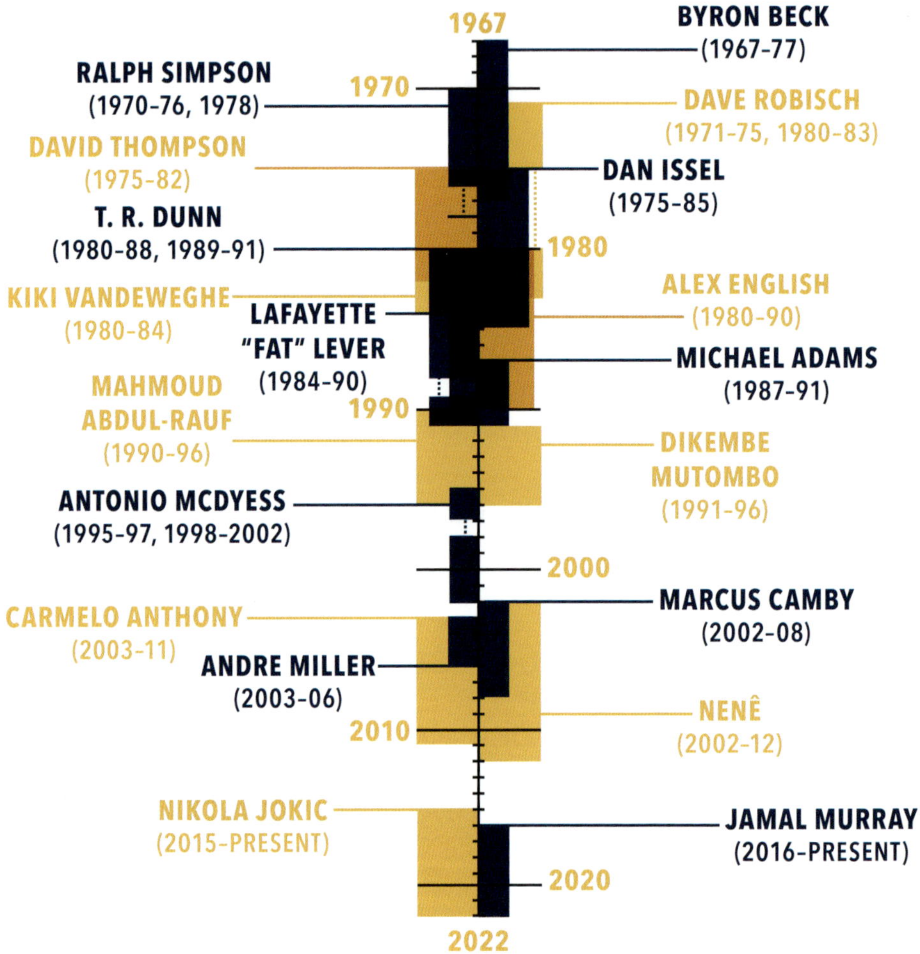
1967
BYRON BECK (1967-77)
RALPH SIMPSON (1970-76, 1978)
1970
DAVE ROBISCH (1971-75, 1980-83)
DAVID THOMPSON (1975-82)
DAN ISSEL (1975-85)
T. R. DUNN (1980-88, 1989-91)
1980
ALEX ENGLISH (1980-90)
KIKI VANDEWEGHE (1980-84)
LAFAYETTE "FAT" LEVER (1984-90)
MICHAEL ADAMS (1987-91)
MAHMOUD ABDUL-RAUF (1990-96)
1990
DIKEMBE MUTOMBO (1991-96)
ANTONIO MCDYESS (1995-97, 1998-2002)
2000
MARCUS CAMBY (2002-08)
CARMELO ANTHONY (2003-11)
ANDRE MILLER (2003-06)
NENÊ (2002-12)
2010
NIKOLA JOKIC (2015-PRESENT)
JAMAL MURRAY (2016-PRESENT)
2020
2022

TEAM FACTS

DENVER NUGGETS

Formerly: Denver Rockets (1967–68 to 1973–74)

First season: 1967–68

NBA championships: 0*

Key coaches:

George Karl (2004–05 to 2012–13)
423–257, 21–38 playoffs

Doug Moe (1980–81 to 1989–90)
432–357, 24–37 playoffs

MORE INFORMATION

To learn more about the Denver Nuggets, go to **pressboxbooks.com/AllAccess.**

These links are routinely monitored and updated to provide the most current information available.

Through 2021–22 season

GLOSSARY

conference
A subset of teams within a sports league.

draft
A system that allows teams to acquire new players coming into a league.

elite
The best of the best.

merged
Combined into one.

rookie
A first-year player.

triple-double
Accumulating 10 or more of three certain statistics in a game.

turnaround
A shot that begins with the shooter's back to the basket.

INDEX

Abdul-Rauf, Mahmoud, 14
Adams, Michael, 12, 14
Anthony, Carmelo, 17–18

Beck, Byron, 5, 7
Brown, Larry, 9

Camby, Marcus, 17

Dunn, T. R., 12

English, Alex, 11–12, 14

Issel, Dan, 8–9, 11

Jokic, Nikola, 21

Karl, George, 21

Lever, Lafayette, 12

McDyess, Antonio, 17
Miller, Andre, 18–19
Moe, Doug, 14, 21
Murray, Jamal, 19, 21
Mutombo, Dikembe, 15, 17

Nenê, 19

Robisch, Dave, 7

Simpson, Ralph, 7

Thompson, David, 7–9

VanDeWeghe, Kiki, 11–12